Congressional Research Service

Social Services Block Grant: Background and Funding

Karen E. Lynch
Specialist in Social Policy

August 28, 2012

Congressional Research Service

7-5700

www.crs.gov

94-953

CRS Report for Congress ———————————————————————
Prepared for Members and Committees of Congress

Summary

The Social Services Block Grant (SSBG) is a flexible source of funds that states use to support a wide variety of social services activities. States have broad discretion over the use of these funds. In FY2009, the most recent year for which expenditure data are available, the largest expenditures for services under the SSBG were for child care, foster care, and special services for the disabled.

The FY2012 Consolidated Appropriations Act (H.R. 2055, P.L. 112-74) provided $1.7 billion for the SSBG in FY2012, the same level of funding as had been requested in the FY2012 President's Budget. This is also the same level of annually appropriated funding that the SSBG has received in every year since FY2002. Since FY2001, annual appropriations for the SSBG have included a provision stipulating that states may transfer up to 10% of their Temporary Assistance for Needy Families (TANF) block grants to the SSBG. In addition to funding from annual appropriations, the SSBG received supplemental appropriations in FY2006 and FY2009 for necessary expenses resulting from natural disasters.

The FY2013 President's Budget, released by the Obama Administration in February 2012, proposed to maintain annual SSBG funding at $1.7 billion. FY2013 appropriations have yet to be enacted, but both the Senate Appropriations Committee-reported bill (S. 3295, S.Rept. 112-176) and the draft bill approved by the House Appropriations Subcommittee on Labor, Health and Human Services, Education, and Related Agencies would maintain level funding for the SSBG.

By contrast, the Sequester Replacement Reconciliation Act of 2012 (H.R. 5652) includes a provision that, if enacted, would repeal the SSBG, effective October 1, 2012. This budget reconciliation bill was agreed to in the House on May 10, 2012, by a vote of 218-199. However, the Senate has not taken up the measure. The House Budget Committee report accompanying the reconciliation bill (H.Rept. 112-470) calls the SSBG a duplicative funding stream that lacks focus and accountability. Those with dissenting views argue that the block grant's flexibility allows states to address the needs of vulnerable populations and respond to local concerns. Prior to the introduction of the reconciliation bill, the House Budget Committee report (H.Rept. 112-421) accompanying the House-passed concurrent resolution on the FY2013 budget (i.e., the House budget resolution for FY2013, H.Con.Res. 112) had included a recommendation that the SSBG be eliminated in FY2013.

Under current law, the SSBG is permanently authorized in Title XX of the Social Security Act (SSA). The 111th Congress amended Title XX of the SSA in the health care reform legislation signed into law by President Obama on March 23, 2010, the Patient Protection and Affordable Care Act (PPACA; P.L. 111-148). This law inserted a new subtitle on elder justice into Title XX, which was itself re-titled as *Block Grants to States for Social Services and Elder Justice*. The health reform law also amended Title XX by establishing two demonstration projects to address the workforce needs of health care professionals and a new competitive grant program to support the early detection of medical conditions related to environmental health hazards. The purpose of this report is to provide background and funding information about the SSBG; the report does not provide detailed information on other programs authorized within Title XX of the SSA.

Contents

Figures

Tables

Appendixes

Contacts

Introduction

The Social Services Block Grant (SSBG) is permanently authorized by Title XX, Subtitle A, of the Social Security Act as a "capped" entitlement to states. This means that states are entitled to their share of funds, as determined by formula, out of an amount of money that is capped in statute at a specific level (also known as a funding ceiling). Although social services for certain welfare recipients have been authorized under various titles of the Social Security Act since 1956, the SSBG in its current form was created in 1981 (P.L. 97-35). Block grant funds are given to states to achieve a wide range of social policy goals, which include promoting self-sufficiency, preventing child abuse, and supporting community-based care for the elderly and disabled.

In FY2012, the SSBG received $1.7 billion from the Consolidated Appropriations Act, 2012 (P.L. 112-74). This is the same amount the Obama Administration had requested for FY2012 and is the same level of annual funding the block grant has received since FY2002. The FY2013 President's Budget would maintain SSBG funding at $1.7 billion. FY2013 appropriations have yet to be enacted, but both the Senate Appropriations Committee-reported bill (S. 3295, S.Rept. 112-176) and the draft bill approved by the House Appropriations Subcommittee on Labor, Health and Human Services, Education, and Related Agencies would maintain $1.7 billion for the SSBG.

By contrast, the committee report (H.Rept. 112-421) accompanying the House-passed concurrent resolution on the FY2013 budget (H.Con.Res. 112) recommended eliminating the SSBG in FY2013.[1] The proposal to repeal the SSBG was ultimately included in a reconciliation package, The Sequester Replacement Reconciliation Act of 2012 (H.R. 5652), which was reported out of the House Budget Committee (H.Rept. 112-470) on May 9, 2012, and agreed to by the House the following day. (See related discussion in the sections on the "FY2013 Budget Resolution and Reconciliation" and the "Proposal to Repeal the SSBG".)

Since FY2001, annual appropriations for the SSBG have included a provision stipulating that states may transfer up to 10% of their Temporary Assistance for Needy Families (TANF) block grants to the SSBG. In addition to funding from annual appropriations, the SSBG has occasionally received supplemental appropriations, including funds that were appropriated for expenses related to natural disasters in FY2006 and FY2009. A special SSBG program for enterprise communities and empowerment zones was authorized in 1993 (P.L. 103-66), but is not currently funded.

Health reform legislation enacted into law (P.L. 111-148) in March 2010 amended Title XX of the Social Security Act to include a subtitle on elder justice and to establish several other programs. Although these changes, briefly discussed later in the report, have technical importance for the statutory citations of the SSBG, they do not substantively amend the provisions within Title XX that govern the SSBG itself. At the federal level, the SSBG is administered by the U.S. Department of Health and Human Services (HHS). Legislation amending Title XX is typically reported by the House Ways and Means Committee and the Senate Finance Committee.

---

[1] H.Rept. 112-421, *Concurrent Resolution on the Budget, FY2013*, March 23, 2012, pp. 89-90.

Use of Funds

Goals

Federal law establishes the five broad goals for the SSBG. Social services funded by states must be linked to one or more of these goals. The five goals are

- achieving or maintaining economic self-support to prevent, reduce, or eliminate dependency;

- achieving or maintaining self-sufficiency, including reduction or prevention of dependency;

- preventing or remedying neglect, abuse, or exploitation of children and adults unable to protect their own interests, or preserving, rehabilitating, or reuniting families;

- preventing or reducing inappropriate institutional care by providing for community-based care, home-based care, or other forms of less intensive care; and

- securing referral or admission for institutional care when other forms of care are not appropriate, or providing services to individuals in institutions.

Services

States have broad discretion in spending SSBG funds to support these broad goals. The following are examples of social services, as specified in law, that relate to the SSBG's broad goals:

> child care, protective services for children and adults, services for children and adults in foster care, services related to the management and maintenance of the home, adult day care, transportation, family planning, training and related services, employment services, referral and counseling services, meal preparation delivery, health support services, and services to meet the special needs of children, the aged, the mentally retarded, the blind, the emotionally disturbed, the physically handicapped, and alcoholics and drug addicts.

In 1993, HHS issued a regulation establishing uniform definitions for 28 SSBG service categories. State spending is not limited to these services; instead, these service categories are used as guidelines for reporting purposes. (Spending on an activity that falls outside the scope of services defined in regulation is characterized under "other services" on annual reports.) In addition to supporting social services, SSBG funds may be used for administration, planning, evaluation, and training. (See **Table 4** for a full list of the service categories reported on by states.) States may also transfer up to 10% of their SSBG allotments to block grants for health activities and low-income home energy assistance.

Prohibited Uses

Although SSBG funds can be used for a broad array of activities, some restrictions are placed on the use of these funds. Funds cannot be used for the following: (1) purchase of land, construction, or major capital improvements; (2) cash payments as a service or for costs of subsistence or room and board (other than costs of subsistence during rehabilitation, temporary emergency shelter provided as a protective service, or in the case of vouchers for certain families as allowed under welfare reform); (3) payment of wages as a social service (except wages of welfare recipients employed in child day care); (4) most medical care (except family planning, rehabilitation services, initial detoxification of certain individuals, or medical care provided as an "integral but subordinate component of a social service"); (5) social services for residents of institutions (including hospitals, nursing homes, and prisons); (6) educational services generally provided by public schools; (7) child care that does not meet applicable state or local standards; (8) services provided by anyone excluded from participation in Medicare or certain other Social Security Act programs; or (9) items or services related to assisted suicide (this provision was added in 1997, under P.L. 105-12).[2] Under extraordinary circumstances, the law does allow HHS to waive two of these prohibitions (use of the SSBG for the purchase of land or capital improvements, or for the provision of medical care).

Eligibility

There are no federal eligibility criteria for SSBG participants. Thus, states have total discretion to set their own eligibility criteria. One exception is that welfare reform established an income limit of 200% of poverty for recipients of services funded by TANF allotments that are transferred to the SSBG.

Allocation of Funds

SSBG funds are allocated to states according to the relative size of each state's population. Grants to Puerto Rico, Guam, the Virgin Islands, and Northern Mariana Islands are based on their share of Title XX funds in FY1981, while grants to American Samoa are based on the relative size of their population compared to the population of the Northern Mariana Islands. No match is required for federal SSBG funds, and federal law does not specify a sub-state allocation formula. In other words, states have complete discretion for the distribution of SSBG funds within their borders. **Table 1** displays FY2012 SSBG allotments by state.

Table 1. Estimated FY2012 SSBG Allotments to States and Territories

State / Territory	Allotment ($)	State / Territory	Allotment ($)
Alabama	26,170,915	Nevada	14,786,568
Alaska	3,888,791	New Hampshire	7,208,186
Arizona	34,998,781	New Jersey	48,139,042
Arkansas	15,965,788	New Mexico	11,274,807
California	203,979,910	New York	106,102,651
Colorado	27,536,806	North Carolina	52,210,481
Connecticut	19,569,572	North Dakota	3,682,698

---

[2] See Section 2005(a) of the Social Security Act.

State / Territory	Allotment ($)	State / Territory	Allotment ($)
Delaware	4,916,538	Ohio	63,166,850
District of Columbia	3,294,668	Oklahoma	20,540,107
Florida	102,944,491	Oregon	20,976,621
Georgia	53,043,671	Pennsylvania	69,550,469
Hawaii	7,448,177	Rhode Island	5,763,214
Idaho	8,583,122	South Carolina	25,325,668
Illinois	70,252,704	South Dakota	4,457,952
Indiana	35,501,340	Tennessee	34,747,395
Iowa	16,679,979	Texas	137,681,734
Kansas	15,621,932	Utah	15,133,346
Kentucky	23,759,723	Vermont	3,426,176
Louisiana	24,821,976	Virginia	43,808,721
Maine	7,273,294	Washington	36,819,474
Maryland	31,612,444	West Virginia	10,145,863
Massachusetts	35,850,817	Wisconsin	31,138,462
Michigan	54,116,776	Wyoming	3,086,072
Minnesota	29,041,054	American Samoa	60,074
Mississippi	16,247,106	Guam	293,103
Missouri	32,791,706	Northern Mariana Islands	58,621
Montana	5,417,432	Puerto Rico	8,793,103
Nebraska	9,999,928	Virgin Islands	293,103

Source: Table prepared by the Congressional Research Service (CRS) based on data from HHS, available online at http://www.acf.hhs.gov/programs/ocs/ssbg/docs/esalloc12.html.

Notes: Figures are based on the annual SSBG appropriation of $1.7 billion, as provided in the FY2012 Consolidated Appropriations Act (P.L. 112-74).

Transfer of TANF Funds to SSBG

The 1996 welfare reform law replaced Aid to Families with Dependent Children (AFDC) with a block grant to states, called Temporary Assistance for Needy Families (TANF), under Title IV-A of the Social Security Act. The law allowed states to transfer up to 10% of their annual TANF allotments into the SSBG. Under provisions of the Transportation Equity Act of 1998 (P.L. 105-178), the amount that states could transfer into SSBG was reduced to 4.25% of their annual TANF allotments, beginning in FY2001. However, this provision was superseded in FY2001 by the FY2001 Consolidated Appropriations Act, which maintained the 10% transfer authority level.

Likewise, the FY2002 appropriations bill presented to the President maintained the 10% transfer authority for FY2002. Earlier, the House had passed its version of a Labor/HHS/Ed appropriations bill (H.R. 3061) proposing to maintain the 10% transfer authority, while the Senate's amended version proposed a 5.7% transfer level. (The Senate Appropriations Committee had recommended a 5.9% transfer authority level in S. 1536; however, the full Senate, in passing an amended H.R. 3061, would have reduced it to 5.7% as a partial offset to funding proposed in S.Amdt. 2084, which provided increased funding for Hispanic education programs.) Ultimately, appropriations acts maintained the transfer authority at 10% in FY2003-FY2012 as well.

There has been some confusion about whether or not the Deficit Reduction Act (DRA, P.L. 109-171) permanently reinstated the 10% transfer authority. This law reauthorized TANF, through the end of FY2010, *in the manner authorized for FY2004.*[3] In that fiscal year, the Social Security Act capped states' authority to transfer TANF funds to the SSBG at 4.25%, but this law was superseded by the FY2004 Consolidated Appropriations Act (P.L. 108-199), which maintained the practice of allowing 10% transfers from TANF to the SSBG. In the wake of the DRA, Congress has continued to ensure that the transfer ceiling stays at 10% by including language to that effect in appropriations legislation.

Over the course of FY1998-FY2011, states annually transferred roughly $1 billion of their TANF funds to the SSBG. In FY2011 alone, 39 states plus the District of Columbia transferred a combined $1.1 billion to the SSBG, with 30 of those states taking advantage of the higher transfer ceiling by moving more than 4.25% of their TANF funds to the SSBG (see **Table A-1** in **Appendix A** for FY2011 state-by-state data).[4] Funds transferred from TANF to the SSBG can be used only for children and families whose income is less than 200% of the federal poverty guidelines. Under welfare reform law, states also may use SSBG funds for vouchers for families that are not eligible for cash assistance because of time limits under the welfare reform program, or for children who are denied cash assistance because they were born into families already receiving benefits for another child.

Funding

FY2013 Appropriations

FY2013 appropriations have yet to be enacted. However, both the House and Senate have initiated the FY2013 appropriations process for the Departments of Labor, Health and Human Services, and Education, and Related Agencies (L-HHS-ED).

On July 18, 2012, the House Appropriations L-HHS-ED Subcommittee approved a bill for full committee consideration. The full committee has yet to consider the bill, but as passed by the subcommittee, the bill would provide $1.7 billion for the SSBG in FY2013.[5]

On June 14, 2012, prior to action in the House, the Senate Appropriations Committee reported a bill to provide full-year FY2013 L-HHS-ED appropriations (S. 3295, S.Rept. 112-176). This bill would also maintain SSBG funding at $1.7 billion for FY2013. In the report accompanying the bill, the Senate Appropriations Committee called the SSBG a "critical source of funding for

---

[3] The conference report for the DRA notes that the House version of the bill increased the maximum transfer to SSBG to 10%, while the Senate bill had no provision. The conference report recedes to the Senate with regard to the transfer authority.

[4] See FY2011 TANF Financial Data available at http://www.acf.hhs.gov/programs/ofs/data/index.html. Calculation is based on FY2011 dollars spent in FY2011; it does not include prior year funds.

[5] Press releases and a draft of the bill released by the subcommittee prior to markup can be found on the House Appropriations Committee website: http://appropriations.house.gov/subcommittees/subcommittee/?IssueID=34777.

services that protect children from neglect and abuse, including providing foster and respite care, as well as related services for children and families, persons with disabilities, and older adults." The report went on to state, "The Committee recognizes the importance of this program, especially in providing mental health and counseling services to underserved populations, and recommends continued usage and flexibility of these funds for such purposes."

Potential Sequestration for FY2013

Readers should note that FY2013 appropriations may be affected by automatic budget reduction procedures (known as "sequestration") authorized by the Budget Control Act of 2011 (BCA, P.L. 112-25).[6] The BCA established a Joint Select Committee on Deficit Reduction, charged with the task of achieving at least $1.2 trillion in deficit reduction over FY2012-FY2021. The Joint Committee did not achieve this goal and Congress has not enacted legislation to repeal or modify the automatic budget reduction procedures. As such, sequestration is currently scheduled to begin on January 2, 2013. At that time, the Office of Management and Budget (OMB) is scheduled to cancel (i.e., sequester) a certain amount of budgetary resources available for FY2013 by reducing non-exempt programs, projects, and activities by a uniform percentage.

For BCA purposes, funding for the SSBG falls into the category of "non-defense mandatory spending" and is not exempt from sequestration.[7] The Congressional Budget Office (CBO) has estimated that budgetary resources for non-defense mandatory programs that are not exempt or subject to special rules would be reduced by roughly 7.8% in FY2013.[8] However, OMB must ultimately determine the actual percentage based on its own interpretations of the law and funding in place at that time. On August 7, 2012, President Obama signed into law the Sequestration Transparency Act of 2012 (P.L. 112-155), which requires the Administration to submit a detailed report to Congress on implementation of sequestration within 30 days of the bill's enactment (i.e., by September 6).

FY2013 Budget Resolution and Reconciliation

On March 29, 2012, the House agreed to a budget resolution for FY2013 (H.Con.Res. 112), which was later deemed enforceable in the House by H.Res 614, as amended by H.Res. 643. The committee report (H.Rept. 112-421) accompanying the House budget resolution for FY2013 included a recommendation that the SSBG be eliminated.[9] In its critique of the SSBG, the committee report noted that states are not required to match federal SSBG allotments or to demonstrate outcomes ("evidence of effectiveness") from their SSBG spending. The report called the SSBG a "duplicative" funding stream, noting that many services supported by the SSBG may also be supported by other federal programs.

---

[6] For a comprehensive discussion of the BCA, see CRS Report R41965, *The Budget Control Act of 2011*, by Bill Heniff Jr., Elizabeth Rybicki, and Shannon M. Mahan.

[7] See CRS Report R42050, *Budget "Sequestration" and Selected Program Exemptions and Special Rules*, coordinated by Karen Spar.

[8] Congressional Budget Office, *Estimated Impact of Automatic Budget Enforcement Procedures Specified in the Budget Control Act*, September 12, 2011, http://www.cbo.gov/publication/42754. See additional CBO materials on the BCA (e.g., estimated impacts, sequestration reports, budget projections) at http://www.cbo.gov/publication/43190.

[9] H.Rept. 112-421, *Concurrent Resolution on the Budget, FY2013*, March 23, 2012, pp. 89-90.

The House budget resolution for FY2013 also included a reconciliation directive requiring certain House authorizing committees to submit deficit reduction recommendations to the House Budget Committee no later than April 27, 2012.[10] On April 18, 2012, the House Ways and Means Committee marked up legislation to comply with the reconciliation directive. The legislation included a proposal, which was agreed to by the committee (22-14), to repeal the SSBG.[11] The legislation was transmitted to the House Budget Committee for inclusion in a larger reconciliation bill.[12] On May 9, 2012, the House Budget Committee reported out the Sequester Replacement Reconciliation Act of 2012 (H.R. 5652, H.Rept. 112-470), which is the reconciliation package that includes the proposal to repeal the SSBG. This bill was passed by the House (218-199) the following day. (For additional information, see related discussion in the section on the "Proposal to Repeal the SSBG".)

The Senate has not agreed to a budget resolution for FY2013. However, on March 20, 2012, Senate Budget Committee Chairman Kent Conrad filed in the *Congressional Record* aggregate spending levels, aggregate revenue levels, and committee spending levels enforceable in the Senate, which have been referred to as a "deeming resolution."[13]

FY2013 Budget Request by the Obama Administration

The Obama Administration released the FY2013 budget on February 13, 2012. The budget requested that funding for the SSBG be maintained at $1.7 billion for FY2013, the same amount it has received annually since FY2002.

FY2012 Appropriations

On December 23, 2011, President Obama signed into law the Consolidated Appropriations Act, 2012 (H.R. 2055, P.L. 112-74), which provided $1.7 billion for the SSBG in FY2012, the same amount of annual funding the block grant has received since FY2002. Prior to the enactment of P.L. 112-74, pro-rated FY2012 funding for the SSBG was provided by three short-term continuing resolutions (P.L. 112-33, P.L. 112-36, and P.L. 112-55), each of which maintained SSBG funding at the annualized level of $1.7 billion.

Before the passage of the first continuing resolution (CR) for FY2012, the House and Senate had initiated the FY2012 appropriations process for L-HHS-ED programs. On September 29, 2011, the House introduced a bill to provide year-long FY2012 L-HHS-ED appropriations (H.R. 3070). This bill would have provided $1.7 billion for the SSBG in FY2012. On September 21, 2011, the Senate Appropriations Committee reported its bill to provide year-long FY2012 L-HHS-ED

---

[10] See Section 201 of H.Con.Res. 112.

[11] For the text of this legislation, visit http://waysandmeans.house.gov/UploadedFiles/041812_3.pdf. Note that the legislation would repeal Title XX-A, Sections 2001-2007, but would not repeal Title XX-B (the subtitle on Elder Justice enacted in health reform legislation) or Sections 2008-2009 of Title XX-A (enacted by health reform legislation to create demonstration projects related to the health care workforce and a competitive grant program for the early detection of medical conditions related to environmental health hazards). For a record of the vote, see http://waysandmeans.house.gov/UploadedFiles/Social_Services_Block_Grant_Roll_Call.pdf.

[12] See reconciliation submissions by committee online at http://budget.house.gov/BudgetAnalysis/Reconciliation.htm.

[13] For more information on deeming resolutions, see CRS Report RL31443, *The "Deeming Resolution": A Budget Enforcement Tool*, by Megan Suzanne Lynch.

appropriations (S. 1599, S.Rept. 112-84). This bill would also have maintained SSBG funding at the $1.7 billion level in FY2012.

FY2012 Budget Resolution

On April 15, 2011, the House passed a concurrent resolution on the FY2012 budget (H.Con.Res. 34), which set broad spending targets for FY2012 and subsequent years. The committee report (H.Rept. 112-58) accompanying the House-passed FY2012 budget resolution included a recommendation that the SSBG be eliminated.[14] In its critique of the SSBG, the committee report noted that states are not required to match federal SSBG allotments or to demonstrate outcomes ("evidence of effectiveness") from their SSBG spending. The report called the SSBG a "duplicative" funding stream, noting that many services supported by the SSBG may also be supported by other federal programs.

FY2012 Budget Request by the Obama Administration

The Obama Administration released the FY2012 Budget on February 14, 2011. The Budget requested that funding for the SSBG be maintained at $1.7 billion for FY2012, the same amount it has received annually since FY2002.

FY2011 Appropriations

Congress did not pass a regular FY2011 appropriations bill for the Departments of Labor, HHS, Education, and Related Agencies. Instead, funding for the SSBG was provided under a series of CRs for the first half of the fiscal year until a final (full-year) FY2011 CR was passed by the Congress and enacted into law (P.L. 112-10) on April 15, 2011. The final FY2011 CR provided $1.7 billion for the SSBG, the same amount of annual funding the block grant has received since FY2002. Seven short-term CRs provided temporary funding for the SSBG prior to the enactment of the final FY2011 CR. Each of these CRs (P.L. 112-8, P.L. 112-6, P.L. 112-4, P.L. 111-322, P.L. 111-317, P.L. 111-290, P.L. 111-242) maintained SSBG funding at the annualized level of $1.7 billion.

Prior to the enactment of the final FY2011 CR, the House had passed alternative legislation (H.R. 1) to extend funding through the end of FY2011, which would have reduced funding for many government programs. However, as passed by the House on February 19, 2011, H.R. 1 would have maintained SSBG funding at the $1.7 billion level. The Senate voted to reject H.R. 1 on March 9, 2011. On March 9, the Senate also voted to reject S.Amdt. 149 to H.R. 1 (in the nature of a substitute), which would have provided full-year funding of $1.7 billion for the SSBG.

Before the passage of the first CR, the House and Senate had initiated the FY2011 L-HHS-ED appropriations process in the 111th Congress. The Senate Subcommittee on L-HHS-ED Appropriations marked up and approved its proposal for FY2011 L-HHS-ED funding on July 27, 2010. The full Senate Appropriations Committee subsequently reported on the proposed FY2011 funding bill (S.Rept. 111-243, S. 3686) on August 2, 2010. This bill would have maintained SSBG funding at the $1.7 billion level. The House Subcommittee on L-HHS-ED Appropriations

---

[14] H.Rept. 112-58, *Concurrent Resolution on the Budget, FY2012*, April 11, 2011, p. 97.

marked up and approved its proposal for FY2011 appropriations on July 15, 2010, but the full House Appropriations Committee took no action on this legislation in the 111th Congress.

FY2011 Budget Request by the Obama Administration

In February 2010, the Obama Administration released the FY2011 Budget, which requested that funding for the SSBG be maintained at $1.7 billion for FY2011, the same amount it has received annually since FY2002.

FY2010 Appropriations

On December 16, 2009, President Obama signed the Consolidated Appropriations Act, 2010, into law as P.L. 111-117. The measure provided $1.7 billion for the SSBG, reflecting the conference report (H.Rept. 111-366) filed on the bill, H.R. 3288, on December 8, 2009. The House and Senate agreed to the conference report on December 10 and December 13, respectively. P.L. 111-117 also maintained the states' authority to transfer up to 10% of their TANF funds to the SSBG.

Prior to the passage of H.R. 3288, both the House and Senate had initiated the L-HHS-ED appropriations process for FY2010. Although the full Senate did not pass a bill to provide L-HHS-ED appropriations for FY2010, the Senate Appropriations Committee did report such a bill (S.Rept. 111-66, H.R. 3293) on August 4, 2009, which sought to maintain funding for the SSBG at the annual level of $1.7 billion. Meanwhile, on July 24, 2009, the House passed its FY2010 L-HHS-ED appropriations bill, H.R. 3293, which also sought to maintain funding for the SSBG at $1.7 billion. Prior to consideration by the full House, this bill was reported by the House Appropriations Committee on July 22, 2009 (H.Rept. 111-220).

FY2010 Budget Request by the Obama Administration

In May 2009, the Obama Administration released the detailed FY2010 Budget, which requested that funding for the SSBG be maintained at $1.7 billion in FY2010. This was a contrast to recent President's Budgets submitted by the Bush Administration, which had proposed funding reductions and, ultimately, full elimination of the SSBG.

FY2009 Appropriations

President Obama signed the FY2009 Omnibus Appropriations Act (P.L. 111-8) into law on March 11, 2009. The FY2009 Omnibus funded the SSBG at an annual level of $1.7 billion in FY2009, rejecting the proposed cuts in the FY2009 budget request submitted by President Bush. The Omnibus also maintained states' authority to transfer up to 10% of their TANF block grants to the SSBG.

Prior to the passage of the FY2009 Omnibus Appropriations Act, Congress had passed two CRs for FY2009 (P.L. 110-329 and P.L. 111-6). Both CRs also rejected cuts proposed by the Bush Administration, maintaining SSBG funding at $1.7 billion. The first of the two CRs (P.L. 110-329) was signed into law by President Bush on September 30, 2008, and remained in effect until March 6, 2009. The second CR (P.L. 111-6) was signed into law by President Obama on March 6, 2009, and lasted until it was superseded by the FY2009 Omnibus on March 11, 2009.

In addition to annual appropriations contained in the FY2009 Omnibus, many programs also received FY2009 funding from the American Recovery and Reinvestment Act of 2009 (ARRA), signed into law by President Obama on February 17, 2009 (P.L. 111-5). The original Senate-passed version of this bill (H.R. 1) would have appropriated $400 million in SSBG funds, to be obligated to states within 60 calendar days from the date at which they become available for obligation. The original House-passed version of H.R. 1, meanwhile, included no funds for SSBG. Ultimately, the enacted version of this legislation adopted the House position on this and, as a result, the SSBG received no supplemental funds from the ARRA.[15]

FY2009 Budget Request by the Bush Administration

President Bush's FY2009 budget, released on February 4, 2008, originally called for $1.2 billion in funding for the SSBG in FY2009, a $500 million decrease from the authorized funding level. However, the Bush Administration subsequently submitted to Congress two amendments to the initial budget request, which combined to reduce the proposed FY2009 SSBG funding level to $0.[16]

In addition to the proposed cut for FY2009, the Bush Administration budget also proposed a plan to permanently eliminate the SSBG beginning in FY2010. The Administration contended that the grant's flexibility and lack of state reporting requirements make it difficult to measure its performance, and that the broad array of services funded through the SSBG often overlap with other federal programs.

Recent Supplemental Appropriations

FY2009 Supplemental Appropriation for Major Disasters of 2008 (and Hurricanes Katrina and Rita)

The first FY2009 CR (P.L. 110-329) included, as Division B, the Disaster Relief and Recovery Supplemental Appropriations Act of 2008. This law provided $600 million in supplemental funds for the SSBG in FY2008. These funds were appropriated on the last day of FY2008 and were not allotted to states by HHS until FY2009. The supplemental funds were appropriated for necessary expenses resulting from "major disasters" (as declared by the President and defined in Title IV of the Stafford Act) occurring during 2008, including hurricanes, floods, and other natural disasters. The appropriation also made these funds available for necessary expenses resulting from Hurricanes Katrina and Rita.

The appropriations language specified that in addition to other uses permitted by Title XX of the Social Security Act, states could use their supplemental SSBG funds to provide social and health services (including mental health services) for individuals, as well as to support the repair, renovation, or construction of health care facilities, mental health facilities, child care centers, and other social services facilities affected by related disasters.

---

[15] For more information about human services programs in the American Recovery and Reinvestment Act, see CRS Report R40211, *Human Services Provisions of the American Recovery and Reinvestment Act*, by Gene Falk et al.

[16] These two amendments to the FY2009 President's Budget can be found on the Government Printing Office (GPO) website at http://www.gpoaccess.gov/USbudget/fy09/amndsup.html (see H.Doc. 110-123 and H.Doc. 110-141).

Allocation of Funds

The appropriations language explicitly required HHS to distribute funding to eligible states based on "demonstrated need in accordance with objective criteria that are made available to the public." HHS outlined their criteria in Information Memorandum Transmittal No. 02-2009, *FY2008 SSBG Supplemental Appropriation of Disaster Assistance Funds Awarded in FY2009*, which was issued by the Department on January 6, 2009.[17] **Figure 1** illustrates how the criteria selected by HHS were used to allocate funds to states.

Figure 1. HHS Allocation Methodology for the FY2009 SSBG Supplemental Funding

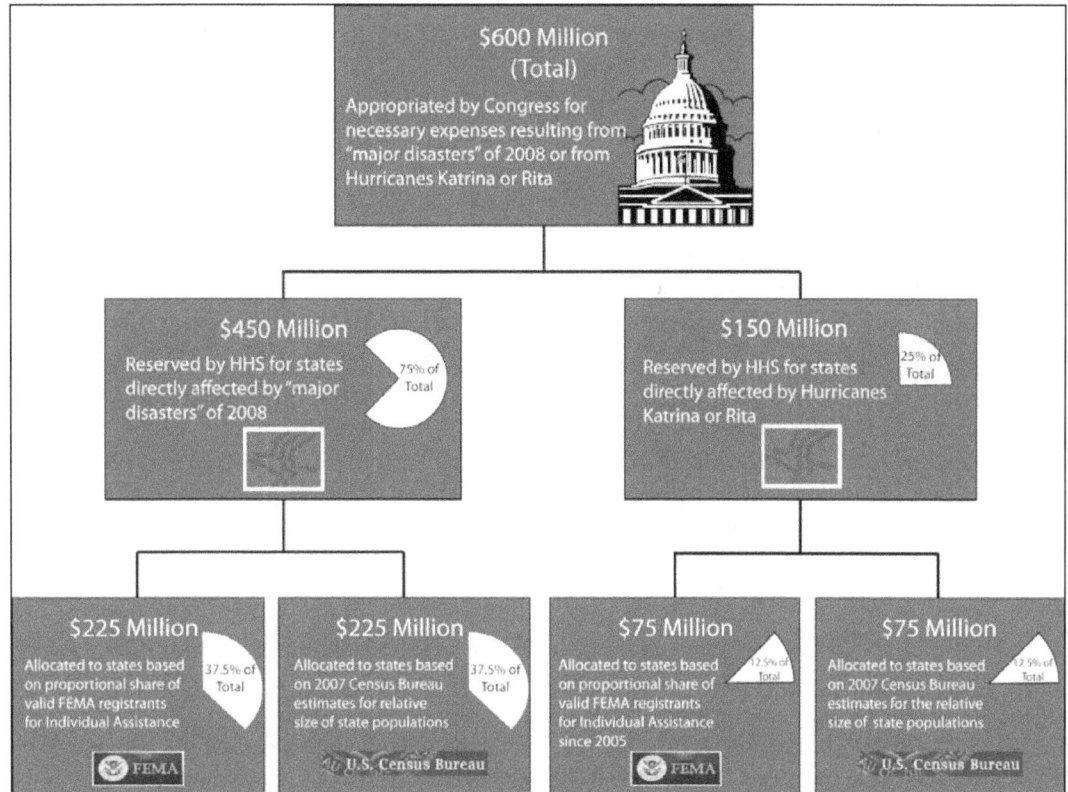

Source: Figure prepared by the Congressional Research Service based on data from HHS.

As specified in the Information Memorandum, HHS identified criteria to determine which disasters qualified for supplemental SSBG funds. First, HHS specified that qualifying major disasters were those that occurred between January 1, 2008, and the date of enactment of the supplemental appropriation (September 30, 2008); in addition, Hurricanes Katrina and Rita were considered to qualify automatically based on appropriations language. Second, HHS restricted qualifying disasters to those which triggered authorizations for Federal Emergency Management Agency (FEMA) Individual Assistance. The FEMA Individual Assistance program provides money or direct assistance to individuals, families, and businesses in an affected area whose property has been damaged or destroyed and whose losses are not covered by insurance. HHS

---

[17] See the Information Memorandum online at http://www.acf.hhs.gov/programs/ocs/ssbg/procedures/IM_0109.html.

chose Individual Assistance data to serve as a proxy for "demonstrated need," noting that these data represent individual households that have declared a loss associated with the disaster and who have registered for assistance.

Twenty states (including the Commonwealth of Puerto Rico) were directly affected by qualifying disasters in 2008, as determined by the HHS criteria. Based on these same criteria, four states were deemed to be eligible for supplemental funds as a result of the lasting effects of Hurricanes Katrina and Rita (all but one of these states had also been affected by disasters in 2008). In total, 21 states (including Puerto Rico) were eligible to receive some share of the $600 million in supplemental funds under the HHS methodology.

As shown in **Figure 1**, the HHS methodology called for three-fourths of the supplemental funds ($450 million) to be reserved for the states that were directly affected by major disasters occurring in 2008. One-fourth of the supplemental ($150 million) was then dedicated to the states facing ongoing needs as a result of Hurricanes Katrina and Rita. From there, funds in each category were allocated to states using two equally weighted sets of data: (1) the proportional share of FEMA registrants for Individual Assistance (that is, individuals from affected communities who validly registered with FEMA after the natural disaster), and (2) the relative size of state populations according to 2007 data from the Census Bureau's American Community Survey. **Table 2** displays the amount allocated to each state.

Expenditure of Funds

Based on data from HHS, states had spent more than $522 million (or 87%) of the $600 million in supplemental funds as of December 15, 2011. As shown in **Table 2**, seven states (Alabama, Indiana, Iowa, Kentucky, Louisiana, Maine, and Mississippi) had spent all of their supplemental funds by that date, while two states (Oklahoma and West Virginia) had not spent any. The remaining states (plus Puerto Rico) had spent some portion of their funds, ranging from 3.5% of Arkansas's allotment to 99.9% of Texas's.

Typically, SSBG funds are subject to a two-year expenditure period—meaning that funds must be spent by the end of the fiscal year subsequent to the fiscal year in which they were allotted to states.[18] The funds from this supplemental were allotted to states in FY2009, giving states until the last day of FY2010 (September 30, 2010) to spend them. However, most states had not spent all of their supplemental funds by the end of FY2010. Recognizing this, Congress passed a bill (S. 3774), which the President signed into law (P.L. 111-285) on November 24, 2010, extending the expenditure deadline for these funds by one fiscal year (to September 30, 2011). Terms and conditions of SSBG grant awards typically give states an additional 90 days (in this case, until December 30, 2011) to liquidate funds that had already been obligated at the end of the fiscal year. Final expenditure data are not yet available.

---

[18] Section 2002(c) of the Social Security Act.

Table 2. State Allocations and Spending from the FY2009 SSBG Supplemental

(as of December 15, 2011)

State	Allocation ($)	Balance ($)	Percent Spent
Alabama	13,092,588	0	100.0%
Arkansas	7,386,653	7,130,072	3.5%
Colorado	8,931,072	6,569,293	26.4%
Florida	35,384,592	20,058,269	43.3%
Georgia	18,111,127	15,909,499	12.2%
Illinois	30,502,439	3,791,646	87.6%
Indiana	18,139,459	0	100.0%
Iowa	11,157,944	0	100.0%
Kentucky	7,732,381	0	100.0%
Louisiana	129,737,880	0	100.0%
Maine	2,425,722	0	100.0%
Mississippi	28,136,577	0	100.0%
Missouri	12,188,291	509,948	95.8%
Nebraska	3,570,592	1,567,285	56.1%
Nevada	4,640,930	1,473,023	68.3%
Oklahoma	6,540,619	6,540,619	0.0%
Puerto Rico	12,427,602	1,364,147	89.0%
Tennessee	11,689,137	4,185,273	64.2%
Texas	218,852,848	218,510	99.9%
West Virginia	3,386,574	3,386,574	0.0%
Wisconsin	15,964,973	5,149,947	67.7%
Total	**600,000,000**	**77,854,157**	**87.0%**

Source: Table prepared by the Congressional Research Service (CRS) based on data from HHS.

FY2006 Supplemental Appropriation for Gulf Coast Hurricanes of 2005

The FY2006 Defense Appropriations Act (P.L. 109-148) included supplemental SSBG funding in the amount of $550 million. These funds were for expenses related to the consequences of the Gulf Coast hurricanes of 2005. The Defense Appropriations Act expanded the potential services for which the additional $550 million could be used to include "health services (including mental health services) and for repair, renovation and construction of health facilities."

Allocation of Funds

Factors used to allocate these supplemental funds included the number of FEMA registrants from hurricanes Katrina, Rita, and Wilma, as well as the percent of individuals in poverty in each state. HHS distributed funds to all states that took in evacuees, not just the states that were directly affected, noting in a February 8, 2006, press release that the Bush Administration had promised no state would be unfairly disadvantaged for providing services to those affected by the storms.[19] Although all states received a portion, Louisiana ($221 million), Mississippi ($128 million), Texas ($88 million), Florida ($54 million), and Alabama ($28 million) received the bulk of funding from the supplemental (94%).

Expenditure of Funds

On May 25, 2007, an FY2007 supplemental appropriations act was signed into law (P.L. 110-28), extending the availability of the supplemental SSBG funds for expenditure through the end of FY2009. In practical terms, this provision gave states until September 30, 2009, to spend all of their supplemental funds.[20] According to HHS, states failed to spend approximately $28.7 million (or about 5%) of the $550 million in supplemental funds prior to the expenditure deadline (see **Table B-1** in **Appendix B** for state-by-state data). This means that about 95% of the supplemental funds were spent prior to the close of FY2009. Unspent funds reverted to the U.S. Treasury.

Additional Funding History

Table 3 shows SSBG funding levels from 1985 on, including the high of $2.8 billion, which was provided annually from FY1991-FY1995. Although $2.8 billion was the originally authorized entitlement ceiling for FY1996, Congress reduced funding to $2.38 billion in that year. Welfare reform legislation (P.L. 104-193) subsequently set the annual SSBG entitlement ceiling at $2.38 billion in each of fiscal years 1997 through 2002. Under the welfare reform law, the ceiling was scheduled to return to a permanent level of $2.8 billion in FY2003.

After welfare reform was enacted, Congress passed an appropriations measure for FY1997 (P.L. 104-208) that contained $2.5 billion for the SSBG, exceeding the ceiling established in the welfare reform law. For FY1998, President Clinton requested that the amount authorized by welfare reform ($2.38 billion) be appropriated. However, Congress approved an FY1998 appropriations bill (P.L. 105-78) containing $2.299 billion for the SSBG. The Senate Appropriations Committee explained the reduction by stating that funding is provided for social services through other federal programs (S.Rept. 105-58). The House Appropriations Committee expressed concern that HHS lacks information on the effectiveness of SSBG-funded activities (H.Rept. 105-205).

In 1998, the Transportation Equity Act (TEA, P.L. 105-178) permanently reduced the SSBG entitlement ceiling to $1.7 billion, beginning in FY2001. However, the entitlement ceiling has not always reflected the actual appropriation. For example, the $1.725 billion appropriation level for FY2001 (H.R. 4577) exceeded the $1.7 billion ceiling by $25 million. In addition, a TEA provision limited the authority for states to transfer TANF funds to the SSBG beginning in FY2001 (reducing the transfer cap from 10%, as established in welfare reform, to 4.25%). However, each annual appropriation from FY2001 onward has included override to reinstate the higher cap, effectively enabling states to transfer up to 10% of their TANF funds to the SSBG.

---

[19] See http://www.hhs.gov/news/press/2006pres/20060208a.html.

[20] The Terms and Conditions of SSBG grant agreements give states 90 days after the end of the grant period to finalize spending for funds they had obligated as of September 30, 2009.

Table 3 shows SSBG entitlement ceilings and appropriations from FY1985-FY2012. Also shown for FY1997-FY2011 are the amounts transferred from TANF to SSBG.

Table 3. SSBG Funding, FY1985-FY2012

(Dollars in billions)

Fiscal Year	Ceiling	Appropriation	Fiscal Year	Ceiling	Appropriation	Transfer from TANF
1985	2.7	2.725[a]	1997	2.380	2.5	0.36
1986	2.7	2.584[b]	1998	2.380	2.299	1.12
1987	2.7	2.7	1999	2.380	1.909	1.32
1988	2.750[c]	2.7	2000	2.380	1.775	1.10
1989	2.7	2.7	2001	1.700	1.725	0.93
1990	2.8	2.762[d]	2002	1.700	1.700	1.03
1991	2.8	2.8	2003	1.700	1.700	0.93
1992	2.8	2.8	2004	1.700	1.700	0.77
1993	2.8	2.8	2005	1.700	1.700	0.92
1994	2.8	2.8	2006	1.700	1.700+0.550[e]	0.97
1995	2.8	2.8	2007	1.700	1.700	1.17
1996	2.381	2.381	2008	1.700	1.700+0.600[f]	1.18
			2009	1.700	1.700	1.21
			2010	1.700	1.700	1.22
			2011	1.700	1.700	1.14
			2012	1.700	1.700	data not yet available

Source: Table prepared by the Congressional Research Service (CRS) based on budget documents and HHS data. In this table, TANF transfer figures reflect data from combined year TANF spending reports; amounts may not necessarily match transfer amounts shown in annual SSBG reports.

a. Amount includes $25 million earmarked for training of daycare providers, licensing officials, and parents, including training in the prevention of child abuse in child care settings (P.L. 98-473).

b. The entitlement ceiling for FY1986 was $2.7 billion. However, the Gramm-Rudman-Hollings legislation sequestration of funds for that period reduced the funding by $116 million.

c. The 1987 Budget Reconciliation Act (P.L. 100-203) included a $50 million increase in the Title XX entitlement ceiling for FY1988; however, these additional funds were not appropriated.

d. The FY1990 appropriation included a supplemental appropriation of $100 million (P.L. 101-198). The Gramm-Rudman-Hollings legislation sequestration of funds for FY1990 reduced funding by $37.8 million to $2.762 billion.

e. The FY2006 Labor-HHS-Education Appropriations Act maintained regular SSBG funding at $1.7 billion. The FY2006 Defense Appropriations Act (P.L. 109-148) provided an additional $550 million in SSBG funding, for necessary expenses related to the consequences of hurricanes in 2005.

f. The Consolidated Appropriations Act, 2008 (P.L. 110-161) maintained regular SSBG funding at $1.7 billion. However, the first FY2009 CR (P.L. 110-329) included, as Division B, the Disaster Relief and Recovery Supplemental Appropriations Act of 2008, which provided $600 million in supplemental SSBG funds. These funds were appropriated on the last day of FY2008, but not allotted to states until FY2009.

State Reporting Requirements

Each year, states are required to submit an intended use plan, often called a "pre-expenditure report," as a prerequisite to receive SSBG funds. The pre-expenditure report must be submitted 30 days prior to the start of the fiscal year.[21] States must also submit a revised report if their planned uses for SSBG funds change during the course of the year. In pre-expenditure reports, states outline their plans for SSBG funds, including the types of services to be supported, and the categories and characteristics of individuals to be served (e.g., children, adults 59 and younger, adults 60 and older, and the disabled).

States are also required to report annually on their actual SSBG expenditures in each of the 29 service categories. For this report, submitted within six months after the end of the reporting period, states use a standard post-expenditure reporting form.[22] HHS published regulations (November 15, 1993) to implement this requirement and to provide states with a uniform set of service category definitions.

States are not required to submit pre-expenditure reports using a standard format like the one required for post-expenditure reporting (e.g., states may simply submit a narrative or chart of their proposed activities and the individuals to be served). However, HHS issued a new Information Memorandum in December 2008, asking states to voluntarily include additional documentation as part of their pre-expenditure reports.[23] Specifically, HHS requested that states submit a copy of the form used for post-expenditure reports, completed with *estimated* (rather than actual) expenditures and recipient data. The reason for this request was to allow for a more accurate analysis of the extent to which states are spending their SSBG funds "in a manner consistent" with their intended use plans. HHS issued a second Information Memorandum on this topic in June 2010, again encouraging states to submit pre-expenditure estimates using the same reporting form that is required for post-expenditure reports.[24]

Most recently, in February 2012, HHS issued an Information Memorandum about a new performance measure that will compare spending plans with actual spending.[25] To support implementation of the performance measure, HHS requested that states submit pre- and post-expenditure reports in Excel using standard reporting forms. HHS also requested that states choosing not to use the standard pre-expenditure reporting form (since the standard form is not technically required) provide a crosswalk to SSBG service categories. In addition, HHS requested that states differentiate in their pre-expenditure reports between estimated spending from the state's SSBG allocation and estimated state spending from projected TANF transfers, because the performance measure will apply only to those funds provided as part of a state's SSBG allocation.

---

[21] This refers to September 1, provided the state operates on a federal fiscal year; alternately, this means June 1 if the state operates on a July-June fiscal year.

[22] See OMB Form No. 0970-0234.

[23] Information Memorandum Transmittal No. 01-2009, *Linking the Social Services Block Grant (SSBG) Pre- and Post-Expenditure Reports*, HHS, Dec. 31, 2008, http://www.acf.hhs.gov/programs/ocs/ssbg/procedures/mema.html.

[24] Information Memorandum Transmittal No. 01-2010, *Pre- and Post-Expenditure Reporting for the SSBG Program*, HHS, June 7, 2010, http://www.acf.hhs.gov/programs/ocs/ssbg/procedures/mema.html.

[25] Information Memorandum Transmittal No. 01-2012, *Implementation of a New Performance Measure*, HHS, February 23, 2012, http://www.acf.hhs.gov/programs/ocs/ssbg/procedures/im12-01.html.

Recent Expenditures

Table 4 shows national SSBG expenditures from FY2009, the most recent year for which SSBG data are available. Expenditures are separated into those made from the annual SSBG allocation and those made from funds transferred from the TANF block grant, and are displayed by service category. In FY2009, the largest expenditures for services under the SSBG were for child care (14%), foster care services for children (13%), and special services for the disabled (11%).

Table 4. Total SSBG Expenditures by Service Category, FY2009

Service Category	SSBG Expenditures Made From:		Total SSBG Expenditures ($)	Percent of Total
	SSBG Allocation ($)	Funds Transferred from TANF ($)		
Adoption Services	21,598,119	23,617,948	45,216,067	2%
Case Management	150,434,644	65,812,653	216,247,297	8%
Congregate Meals	7,173,962	8,884	7,182,846	0%
Counseling Services	20,642,121	3,028,957	23,671,078	1%
Day Care—Adults	23,988,382	21,589	24,009,971	1%
Day Care—Children	110,401,462	280,212,803	390,614,264	14%
Education and Training Services	21,632,305	2,257,017	23,889,322	1%
Employment Services	11,361,657	1,262,902	12,624,559	0%
Family Planning Services	12,207,117	21,487,705	33,694,822	1%
Foster Care Services— Adults	29,577,968	8,438,347	38,016,314	1%
Foster Care Services— Children	132,657,642	240,167,267	372,824,909	13%
Health-Related Services	16,549,569	1,794,449	18,344,018	1%
Home-Based Services	169,380,683	28,184,628	197,565,311	7%
Home-Delivered Meals	25,482,489	48,919	25,531,408	1%
Housing Services	10,977,151	7,252,176	18,229,327	1%
Independent/Transitional Living	6,794,858	1,073,922	7,868,780	0%
Information and Referral	17,478,571	4,259,729	21,738,300	1%
Legal Services	18,287,739	844,415	19,132,154	1%
Pregnancy and Parenting	7,723,212	2,046,509	9,769,720	0%
Prevention and Intervention	44,392,821	88,959,481	133,352,303	5%
Protective Services— Adults	210,302,566	5,423,422	215,725,988	8%
Protective Services— Children	133,001,497	137,159,212	270,160,708	10%
Recreation Services	746,800	146,103	892,903	0%

	SSBG Expenditures Made From:			
Service Category	**SSBG Allocation ($)**	**Funds Transferred from TANF ($)**	**Total SSBG Expenditures ($)**	**Percent of Total**
Residential Treatment	58,881,865	47,642,297	106,524,162	4%
Special Services—Disabled	243,419,274	71,447,923	314,867,196	11%
Special Services—Youth at Risk	20,820,932	4,632,124	25,453,056	1%
Substance Abuse Services	4,504,880	966,279	5,471,159	0%
Transportation	20,107,583	2,755,929	22,863,512	1%
Other Services	98,220,448	51,254,759	149,475,207	5%
Administrative Costs	74,774,141	15,701,228	90,475,369	3%
Total SSBG Expenditures	**1,723,522,458**	**1,117,909,571**	**2,841,432,029**	**100%**

Source: Table prepared by CRS based on data included in the Social Services Block Grant Program Annual Report 2009 (note that TANF transfer data from this source may differ from data in TANF financial reports). Full report available at http://www.acf.hhs.gov/programs/ocs/ssbg/reports/reports.html.

Note: Totals may not sum due to rounding.

Recent Legislative Action

Other than appropriations legislation, no bills in the 109th Congress or 110th Congress that proposed changes to the SSBG were enacted into law. During the first session of the 111th Congress, several bills were introduced (S. 795, H.R. 2006, S. 1796, H.R. 3590) which sought to amend Title XX of the Social Security Act (SSA)—the authorizing statute for the SSBG—to establish new programs to address the prevention, detection, and treatment of elder abuse or elder justice. Ultimately, the health care reform legislation passed by Congress in March 2010 included three provisions amending Title XX of the SSA (addressed briefly below), including one on elder justice. More recently, within the 112th Congress, there has been consideration of a proposal to repeal the SSBG.

Proposal to Repeal the SSBG

On May 10, 2012, the House passed the Sequester Replacement Reconciliation Act of 2012 (H.R. 5652) by a recorded vote of 218-199. This bill includes a provision (Section 621) that, if enacted, would repeal the SSBG, effective October 1, 2012. The Senate has not taken up the measure.

The Sequester Replacement Reconciliation Act of 2012 (H.R. 5652) is a budget reconciliation bill. Budget reconciliation is an optional process that may be used by Congress to bring existing spending, revenue, and debt-limit laws into compliance with fiscal priorities established in the annual budget resolution.[26] The FY2013 House budget resolution included a reconciliation

---

[26] For more information about budget reconciliation, see CRS Report R41186, *Reconciliation Directives: Components* (continued...)

directive in Section 201. To comply with this directive, on April 18, 2012, the House Ways and Means Committee marked up legislation to meet its deficit reduction targets. This legislation included a provision to repeal the SSBG that was agreed to by the committee by a vote of 22-14.[27] The House Budget Committee compiled this legislation, along with submissions from other House committees, into the Sequester Replacement Reconciliation Act of 2012 and reported the bill out of committee (H.Rept. 112-470) on May 9, 2012.[28]

The report accompanying the Sequester Replacement Reconciliation Act of 2012 (H.Rept. 112-470) includes text explaining the decision to repeal the SSBG.[29] The report calls the SSBG a duplicative funding stream that lacks focus and accountability. The report also criticizes the SSBG for not requiring states to match federal SSBG allotments. Committee reports accompanying House budget resolutions for the past two years have included similar critiques of the SSBG and, in each year, have recommended that the program be eliminated.[30] Similar arguments had previously been made by the George W. Bush Administration in proposing, as part of annual budget requests, to reduce and eventually eliminate funding for the SSBG.[31]

The committee report also includes a summary of dissenting views, which focuses largely on how the elimination of the SSBG might affect the vulnerable individuals served by these funds.[32] These arguments are similar to concerns put forward by other critics of the proposal to eliminate the SSBG, such as the National Conference of State Legislatures (NCSL).[33] The NCSL, for instance, has argued that the flexible nature of the SSBG allows states to address the needs of vulnerable populations and respond to local concerns and that eliminating the SSBG might shift costs of such services directly to states.[34]

(...continued)

and Enforcement, by Megan Suzanne Lynch.

[27] For the text of this legislation, visit http://waysandmeans.house.gov/UploadedFiles/041812_3.pdf. Note that the legislation would repeal Title XX-A, Sections 2001-2007, but would not repeal Title XX-B (the subtitle on Elder Justice enacted in health reform legislation) or Sections 2008-2009 of Title XX-A (enacted by health reform legislation to create demonstration projects related to the health care workforce and a competitive grant program for the early detection of medical conditions related to environmental health hazards).

[28] See reconciliation submissions by committee online at http://budget.house.gov/BudgetAnalysis/Reconciliation.htm.

[29] See text beginning on p. 505 of H.Rept. 112-470.

[30] For FY2013, see H.Rept. 112-421, *Concurrent Resolution on the Budget, FY2013*, March 23, 2012, pp. 89-90. For FY2012, see H.Rept. 112-58, *Concurrent Resolution on the Budget, FY2012*, April 11, 2011, p. 97.

[31] See discussion of these proposals in budget justifications of the HHS Administration for Children and Families, available online at http://transition.acf.hhs.gov/programs/olab/budget. The FY2007 and FY2008 President's Budgets proposed to reduce funding for the SSBG, but not permanently eliminate the program. The initial FY2009 President's Budget proposed to decrease funding for the SSBG by $500 million in FY2009, but to permanently eliminate the program beginning in FY2010. Subsequent amendments to the President's Budget reduced the FY2009 request to $0. For additional details on the FY2009 request, see the "FY2009 Budget Request by the Bush Administration" section.

[32] H.Rept. 112-470, pp. 539-540.

[33] Letter from The Honorable Tom Hansen (South Dakota Senate) and The Honorable Barbara W. Ballard (Kansas House of Representatives), Chairs of the NCSL Human Services and Welfare Committee, to The Honorable David Camp and the Honorable Sander Levin, Chair and Ranking Member (respectively) of the House Committee on Ways and Means, April 16, 2012, http://www.ncsl.org/issues-research/human-services/ncsl-letter-opposing-permanent-elimination-of-ssbg.aspx. See also Indivar Dutta-Gupta, LaDonna Pavetti, and Ife Finch, *Eliminating Social Services Block Grant Would Weaken Services for Vulnerable Children, Adults, and Disabled*, Center on Budget and Policy Priorities, May 3, 2012, http://www.cbpp.org/cms/index.cfm?fa=view&id=3765#_ftnref11.

[34] Ibid.

How Did Health Reform Affect the SSBG?

On March 23, 2010, President Obama signed into law a comprehensive health care reform bill, the Patient Protection and Affordable Care Act (PPACA; P.L. 111-148). This law included three provisions that amended the SSBG's authorizing legislation, Title XX of the SSA. These provisions, discussed briefly below, created new programs related to elder justice, the health care workforce, and environmental health hazards. Notably, these changes were primarily of technical importance with respect to the SSBG. That is, they affected statutory citations for the SSBG, but they did not substantively amend the provisions within Title XX that govern the SSBG itself.

New Subtitle on Elder Justice

The health reform law re-titled Title XX as *Block Grants to States for Social Services and Elder Justice* (formerly, Title XX was entitled *Block Grants to States for Social Services*). The law also divided Title XX into two subtitles: Subtitle A retained provisions related to the SSBG, while Subtitle B comprised a series of new provisions related to elder justice.[35] The elder justice provisions established (1) an Elder Justice Coordinating Council; (2) an Advisory Board on Elder Abuse, Neglect, and Exploitation; (3) a new grant program for stationary and mobile forensic centers to develop forensic expertise pertaining to elder abuse, neglect, and exploitation; and (4) several new grant programs (and other activities) to promote elder justice.[36]

New Programs Authorized within the SSBG Subtitle of Title XX

The health care reform law (P.L. 111-148) also included provisions establishing two new sections within Subtitle A of Title XX. The first created two demonstration projects related to the health care workforce. The second called for HHS to establish a competitive grant program for the early detection of medical conditions related to environmental health hazards. The health reform law established these new programs within the SSBG subtitle of Title XX and subjected their funding to the same prohibited uses as SSBG funds (though the new law made two exceptions[37] to this rule). However, these new programs do not substantively alter the SSBG itself. The funding for these programs was provided separately in the health reform law (through mandatory pre-appropriations) and is not subject to the SSBG allocation formula.

---

[35] See Sections 6701-6703 of the Patient Protection and Affordable Care Act (PPACA, P.L. 111-148).

[36] A full description of these provisions is beyond the scope of this report, which is focused on the SSBG. For a summary of the provisions in P.L. 111-148 related to elder justice, see CRS Report R40943, *Public Health, Workforce, Quality, and Related Provisions in the Patient Protection and Affordable Care Act (P.L. 111-148)*, coordinated by C. Stephen Redhead and Erin D. Williams.

[37] Section 10323(b) of PPACA (P.L. 111-148) specifies that the general prohibition against using SSBG funds for the provision of medical care shall not be construed as to prohibit recipients of a grant for the early detection of medical conditions related to environmental health hazards from conducting screening for environmental health conditions. In addition, Section 5507 of PPACA exempts both health care workforce demonstrations projects from the prohibition against using SSBG funds for the provision of an education service that the state makes generally available to its residents without cost and without regard to their income.

Additional Legislative History

Proposals to increase funding for the SSBG were included as part of welfare reauthorization bills in the 109th Congress, but these were not passed. (S. 667 would have increased funding for the SSBG by $1 billion over five years, and both H.R. 751 and S. 6 would have provided $1.975 billion for the SSBG in FY2006 and $2.8 billion in FY2007.) Instead, a scaled-back version of welfare reauthorization, which included none of the SSBG provisions, was included in reconciliation legislation and signed into law (P.L. 109-171) on February 8, 2006.

Appendix A. TANF Transfers to SSBG in FY2011

Table A-1. TANF Transfers to the SSBG in FY2011

State	Total Federal TANF Funds[a] ($)	TANF Funds Transferred to SSBG[b] ($)	Percent of TANF Funds Transferred to SSBG	SSBG Allocation ($)	Total SSBG Funds With TANF Transfer ($)
Alabama	100,653,578	8,964,633	8.91%	25,928,224	34,892,857
Alaska	49,816,731	4,981,673	10.00%	3,846,101	8,827,774
Arizona	215,968,002	21,596,800	9.56%	36,319,265	57,916,065
Arkansas	60,846,417	0	0.00%	15,910,587	15,910,587
California	3,659,389,581	340,460,690	9.30%	203,527,234	543,987,924
Colorado	145,033,266	16,216,068	10.68%	27,668,480	43,884,548
Connecticut	266,788,107	26,678,810	10.00%	19,373,246	46,052,056
Delaware	32,290,981	-3,229,098	-9.52%	4,873,872	1,644,774
District of Columbia	92,609,815	3,935,917	4.05%	3,301,976	7,237,893
Florida	602,299,471	60,229,946	10.00%	102,078,238	162,308,184
Georgia	355,405,213	0	0.00%	54,123,974	54,123,974
Hawaii	98,904,788	9,890,000	9.52%	7,131,822	17,021,822
Idaho	32,726,579	3,272,658	10.00%	8,511,862	11,784,520
Illinois	585,056,960	7,915,460	1.35%	71,090,410	79,005,870
Indiana	206,799,109	0	0.00%	35,368,495	35,368,495
Iowa	131,030,394	12,962,008	9.89%	16,562,583	29,524,591
Kansas	101,931,061	10,193,106	9.52%	15,521,265	25,714,371
Kentucky	181,287,669	0	0.00%	23,755,410	23,755,410
Louisiana	175,235,636	16,397,199	9.36%	24,735,353	41,132,552
Maine	78,120,889	0	0.00%	7,259,147	7,259,147
Maryland	229,098,032	22,909,803	9.52%	31,383,841	54,293,644
Massachusetts	459,371,116	45,937,113	9.52%	36,307,200	82,244,313
Michigan	775,352,858	77,535,285	9.52%	54,897,717	132,433,002
Minnesota	263,434,070	4,790,000	1.82%	28,998,098	33,788,098
Mississippi	92,744,827	9,274,483	10.00%	16,254,993	25,529,476
Missouri	217,051,740	21,701,176	10.00%	32,970,258	54,671,434
Montana	38,788,416	1,998,226	5.15%	5,368,720	7,366,946
Nebraska	57,513,601	0	0.00%	9,892,977	9,892,977
Nevada	46,377,313	754,063	1.55%	14,553,992	15,308,055
New Hampshire	38,521,261	936,937	2.43%	7,293,695	8,230,632
New Jersey	404,034,823	16,938,000	3.99%	47,948,654	64,886,654

State	Total Federal TANF Funds[a] ($)	TANF Funds Transferred to SSBG[b] ($)	Percent of TANF Funds Transferred to SSBG	SSBG Allocation ($)	Total SSBG Funds With TANF Transfer ($)
New Mexico	114,913,087	0	0.00%	11,066,135	11,066,135
New York	2,442,930,602	192,797,333	7.52%	107,603,864	300,401,197
North Carolina	326,126,929	10,311,313	3.02%	51,655,287	61,966,600
North Dakota	26,399,809	0	0.00%	3,561,809	3,561,809
Ohio	727,968,260	43,260,642	5.94%	63,558,897	106,819,539
Oklahoma	145,281,442	14,528,144	10.00%	20,302,524	34,830,668
Oregon	166,798,629	0	0.00%	21,065,756	21,065,756
Pennsylvania	719,499,305	30,977,000	4.31%	69,407,410	100,384,410
Rhode Island	95,021,587	7,557,672	7.95%	5,799,434	13,357,106
South Carolina	99,967,824	0	0.00%	25,116,211	25,116,211
South Dakota	21,279,651	2,127,965	10.00%	4,473,339	6,601,304
Tennessee	205,789,495	0	0.00%	34,669,953	34,669,953
Texas	521,123,819	32,408,086	6.22%	136,462,292	168,870,378
Utah	81,367,577	2,445,999	3.01%	15,333,082	17,779,081
Vermont	47,353,181	4,735,318	10.00%	3,423,685	8,159,003
Virginia	158,285,172	12,648,498	7.99%	43,405,019	56,053,517
Washington	380,544,968	10,702,000	2.68%	36,695,999	47,397,999
West Virginia	110,176,310	11,017,631	10.00%	10,020,495	21,038,126
Wisconsin	314,499,354	14,837,318	4.49%	31,137,681	45,974,999
Wyoming	18,500,530	1,850,053	10.00%	2,996,991	4,847,044
Total	**16,518,309,835**	**1,135,445,928**	**-**	**1,690,513,552**	**2,825,959,480**

Source: Table prepared by the Congressional Research Service (CRS) based on FY2011 data reported by HHS. In this table, TANF financial data reflect FY2011 one-year (not combined) spending, whereas SSBG figures represent FY2011 allocations. TANF financial data are available online at http://www.acf.hhs.gov/programs/ofs/data/index.html.

a. Amounts in this column reflect FY2011 state financial assistance grants and supplemental grants to states, but do not include contingency funds or tribal grants (see Table E2a of FY2011 TANF financial data).

b. The amounts in this column is the total amount of FY2011 TANF funding transferred to the SSBG in FY2011; it does not include any adjustments made for previous years (see Table A6 of FY2011 TANF financial data). Funds transferred back to the TANF program that were not obligated and liquidated within the program deadlines are reported as negative amounts.

Appendix B. FY2006 Supplemental SSBG Funding

The FY2006 Defense Appropriations Act (P.L. 109-148) included $550 million in supplemental SSBG funding for expenses related to the consequences of the Gulf Coast hurricanes of 2005. **Table B-1** displays state-by-state allocations and balances (i.e., unspent funds) from the FY2006 supplemental. These HHS data suggest that approximately $28.7 million (or 5%) of the supplemental funds were not spent before the expenditure deadline of September 30, 2009. Unspent funds reverted to the U.S. Treasury.

Table B-1. State Spending from the FY2006 SSBG Supplemental

(as reported on April 1, 2010)

State	Allocation ($)	Balance ($) (Amount Unspent)	Percent Spent
Alabama	27,852,254	16,601	99.94%
Alaska	37,554	37,554	0.00%
Arizona	487,931	182,722	62.55%
Arkansas	3,603,505	2,780,335	22.84%
California	3,051,021	1,945,928	36.22%
Colorado	545,168	112,876	79.30%
Connecticut	113,858	0	100.00%
Delaware	39,178	0	100.00%
District of Columbia	328,256	0	100.00%
Florida	53,808,916	16,446,605	69.44%
Georgia	6,325,537	1,245,651	80.31%
Hawaii	34,153	34,153	0.00%
Idaho	35,224	12,794	63.68%
Illinois	1,351,677	2,942	99.78%
Indiana	381,125	231,653	39.22%
Iowa	126,200	43,966	65.16%
Kansas	191,975	0	100.00%
Kentucky	525,110	0	100.00%
Louisiana	220,901,534	179,382	99.92%
Maine	67,995	3	100.00%
Maryland	380,188	1,899	99.50%
Massachusetts	331,948	284,422	14.32%
Michigan	734,927	134,889	81.65%
Minnesota	153,936	86,135	44.04%
Mississippi	128,398,427	0	100.00%
Missouri	797,091	0	100.00%
Montana	41,786	41,786	0.00%

State	Allocation ($)	Balance ($) (Amount Unspent)	Percent Spent
Nebraska	114,925	0	100.00%
Nevada	273,291	217,884	20.27%
New Hampshire	23,717	23,717	0.00%
New Jersey	259,599	0	100.00%
New Mexico	265,277	265,277	0.00%
New York	1,182,346	1,182,346	0.00%
North Carolina	1,310,272	578,271	55.87%
North Dakota	13,009	0	100.00%
Ohio	556,283	496,967	10.66%
Oklahoma	932,353	932,353	0.00%
Oregon	177,170	0	100.00%
Pennsylvania	402,568	41,436	89.71%
Rhode Island	69,382	0	100.00%
South Carolina	696,901	234,866	66.30%
South Dakota	21,624	0	100.00%
Tennessee	3,470,718	0	100.00%
Texas	87,951,690	0	100.00%
Utah	92,669	19	99.98%
Vermont	23,272	23,272	0.00%
Virginia	808,855	808,855	0.00%
Washington	326,206	0	100.00%
West Virginia	132,912	31,233	76.50%
Wisconsin	227,555	9,094	96.00%
Wyoming	20,932	20,932	0.00%
Total	**550,000,000**	**28,688,818**	**94.78%**

Source: Table prepared by the Congressional Research Service (CRS) based on data from HHS.

Notes: These funds were appropriated in the FY2006 Defense Appropriations Act (P.L. 109-148). A supplemental appropriations act for FY2007 (P.L. 110-28) extended the expenditure deadline for these funds, giving states until the end of FY2009 (September 30, 2009) to spend their allotments. Under the Terms and Conditions of their grant agreements, states had 90 days after the end of the grant period to finalize spending for funds that were obligated as of September 30, 2009. The numbers above (reported on April 1, 2010) should reflect final expenditures from the FY2006 supplemental. By law, unspent funds revert to the U.S. Treasury.

Author Contact Information

Karen E. Lynch
Specialist in Social Policy
klynch@crs.loc.gov, 7-6899

www.ingramcontent.com/pod-product-compliance
Lightning Source LLC
Chambersburg PA
CBHW080109010626
45794CB00015B/3410